LET'S PLAY FLUTE!

COMPANION TO LET'S PLAY FLUTE! METHOD BOOK 1

by Elisabeth Weinzierl & Edmund Waechter

Repertoire Correlates to
Let's Play Flute! Method Book 1
50600096

To access companion recorded accompaniments online, visit:
www.halleonard.com/mylibrary

Enter Code
3500-7234-2752-9471

If you require a physical CD of the online audio that accompanies this book, please contact Hal Leonard Corporation at info@halleonard.com.

Sy. 2925

RICORDI

HAL•LEONARD®
CORPORATION
7777 W. BLUEMOUND RD. P.O. BOX 13819 MILWAUKEE, WI 53213

www.halleonard.com

PREFACE

Let's Play Flute...

...and have fun making music with others! Learning the fundamentals of ensemble playing should accompany and enrich private instrumental instruction from the very beginning. In addition to being fun, the pedagogical importance of emphasizing chamber music techniques cannot be overstated. Rhythmic stability and intonation are naturally improved through ensemble playing, as are the ability to listen to others and react to them.

For this repertoire book, we have chosen twenty-three songs, dances, character pieces, and classical melodies from various time periods and countries, that flute students are able to master quickly. The piano part has been arranged at a similar level of difficulty, so that two musicians of around the same age and/or level of experience may play together. Accompaniment recordings of the piano part give students the opportunity to practice with piano, even when a pianist is not available. For the faster pieces, both a slow tempo and a fast tempo accompaniment recording are provided.

—Elisabeth Weinzierl and Edmund Waechter

Some pieces have two accompaniment recordings. One is at a slower practice tempo,
and the other is at a performance tempo. These are clearly indicated throughout.

TABLE OF CONTENTS

Repertoire correlates to *Method Book 1*

This table of contents is organized by the corresponding chapters in *Let's Play Flute! Method Book 1*. In addition, at the bottom of each page in this book, you will find a note that tells you from which chapter you will be able to play each piece. For example, if the bottom of the page states "*Let's Play Flute! Method Book 1,* Chapter 6," you will have learned all the notes for the piece once you have finished Chapter 6 in *Let's Play Flute! Method Book 1*.

Pavane and Galliard

Claude Gervaise (c1510 – c1558)
Arr.: E. Weinzierl / E. Waechter

Let's Play Flute! Method Book 1, Chapter 6   Sy. 2925   © 2015 by G. Ricordi & Co., Berlin

Brazilian Folksong

Practice tempo: Moderato
Performance tempo: Allegro

Arr.: E. Weinzierl / E. Waechter

Moderato

Samuel Maykapar (1867–1938)
Arr.: E. Weinzierl / E. Waechter

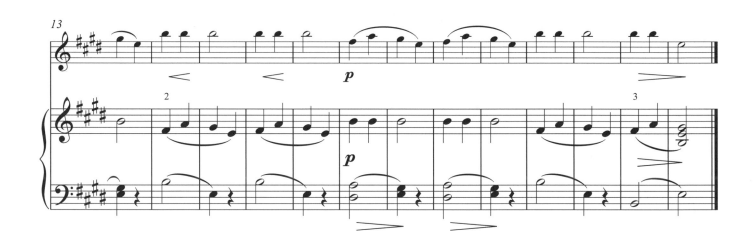

Scherzo
Op. 149, No. 6

Anton Diabelli (1781–1858)
Arr.: E. Weinzierl / E. Waechter

Practice tempo: Moderato
Performance tempo: Allegro

Sy. 2925

Hungarian Song
Op. 44, No. 2

Edmund Parlow (1855–unknown)
Arr.: E. Weinzierl / E. Waechter

Sy. 2925

Sascha

Russian Folksong
Arr.: E. Weinzierl / E. Waechter

Careless Hans

Daniel Gottlob Türk (1750–1830)
Arr.: E. Weinzierl / E. Waechter

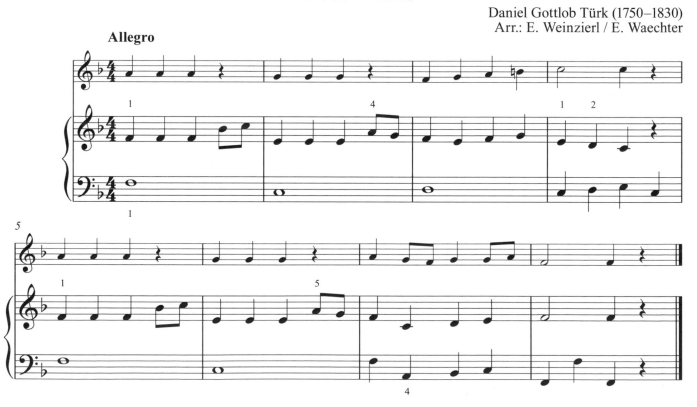

There is a b-flat in the key signature, but it is never played. There is a b-natural in measure three. Therefore, use the single thumb key.

Sy. 2925

Samba

Practice tempo: Moderato
Performance tempo: Allegro

Brazilian Folksong
Arr.: E. Weinzierl / E. Waechter

Sy. 2925

Presto
Op. 87, No. 35

Heinrich Wohlfahrt (1797–1883)
Arr.: E. Weinzierl / E. Waechter

Practice tempo: Moderato
Performance tempo: Allegro

D.C. al Fine

Romanian Song

Arr.: E. Weinzierl / E. Waechter

Sy. 2925

Pretty Minka

Russian Song
Arr.: E. Weinzierl / E. Waechter

Sy. 2925

Mary and Martha

African-American Spiritual
Arr.: E. Weinzierl / E. Waechter

Sleigh Ride
from KV 605

Wolfgang Amadeus Mozart (1756–1791)
Arr.: E. Weinzierl / E. Waechter

Chichico

Brazilian Song
Arr.: E. Weinzierl / E. Waechter

Practice tempo: Allegro moderato
Performance tempo: Allegro

Percussive Tones (beat boxing)

Sy. 2925

Allegro
Op. 149, No. 13

Anton Diabelli (1781–1858)
Arr.: E. Weinzierl / E. Waechter

Practice tempo: Moderato
Performance tempo: Allegro

* Use the rests to slide to the other thumb key: Start with the double thumb key (DTK), change to the single thumb key (STK) in measure eight, and switch back to the double thumb key in measure sixteen.

Allegro

Johann Baptist Vanhal (1739–1831)
Arr.: E. Weinzierl / E. Waechter

Practice tempo: Moderato
Performance tempo: Allegro

* To ease breathing, leave out the notes in parentheses.

Sy. 2925

LET'S PLAY FLUTE!

COMPANION TO LET'S PLAY FLUTE! METHOD BOOK 1

by Elisabeth Weinzierl & Edmund Waechter

Repertoire Correlates to
Let's Play Flute! Method Book 1
50600096

To access companion recorded accompaniments online, visit **www.halleonard.com/mylibrary**
and enter the access code printed on the title page of the flute/piano score.

Some pieces have two accompaniment recordings. One is at a slower practice tempo,
and the other is at a performance tempo. These are clearly indicated throughout.

Sy. 2925

RICORDI

HAL•LEONARD®
CORPORATION

7777 W. BLUEMOUND RD. P.O. BOX 13819 MILWAUKEE, WI 53213

Original publication: *Flöte Spielen Spielbuch A*, by Elisabeth Weinzierl and Edmund Waechter (Sy. 2941)
© 2013 by G. Ricordi & Co.
All rights reserved

English translation/adaptation: *Let's Play Flute! Repertoire Book 1*, by Elisabeth Weinzierl and Edmund Waechter
English translation/adaptation by Rachel Kelly
© 2015 by G. Ricordi & Co.
All rights reserved
Exclusively distributed by Hal Leonard MGB, a Hal Leonard Corporation company.

www.halleonard.com

TABLE OF CONTENTS

This table of contents is organized by the corresponding chapters in *Let's Play Flute! Method Book 1*. In addition, at the bottom of each page in this book, you will find a note that tells you from which chapter you will be able to play each piece. For example, if the bottom of the page states "*Let's Play Flute! Method Book 1,* Chapter 6," you will have learned all the notes for the piece once you have finished Chapter 6 in *Let's Play Flute! Method Book 1*.

The price of this publication includes access to companion recorded accompaniments online, for download or streaming, using the unique code found on the title page of the piano score. Visit **www.halleonard.com/mylibrary** and enter the access code.

Flute

Pavane and Galliard

Claude Gervaise (c1510 – c1558)
Arr.: E. Weinzierl / E. Waechter

Larghetto
Pavane

Galliard

Let's Play Flute! Method Book 1, Chapter 6   Sy. 2925   © 2015 by G. Ricordi & Co., Berlin

Brazilian Folksong

Practice tempo: Moderato
Performance tempo: Allegro

Arr.: E. Weinzierl / E. Waechter

Let's Play Flute! Method Book 1, Chapter 8   Sy. 2925   © 2015 by G. Ricordi & Co., Berlin

4

Moderato

Samuel Maykapar (1867–1938)
Arr.: E. Weinzierl / E. Waechter

Scherzo
Op. 149, No. 6

Practice tempo: Moderato
Performance tempo: Allegro

Anton Diabelli (1781–1858)
Arr.: E. Weinzierl / E. Waechter

Hungarian Song
Op. 44, No. 2

Allegro con fuoco

Edmund Parlow (1855–unkown)
Arr.: E. Weinzierl / E. Waechter

Sy. 2925

6

Sascha

Russian Folksong
Arr.: E. Weinzierl / E. Waechter

Careless Hans

Daniel Gottlob Türk (1750–1830)
Arr.: E. Weinzierl / E. Waechter

There is a b-flat in the key signature, but it is never played. There is a b-natural in measure three. Therefore, use the single thumb key.

Samba

Brazilian Folksong
Arr.: E. Weinzierl / E. Waechter

Practice tempo: Moderato
Performance tempo: Allegro

Presto
Op. 87, No. 35

Heinrich Wohlfahrt (1797–1883)
Arr.: E. Weinzierl / E. Waechter

Practice tempo: Moderato
Performance tempo: Allegro

p

Fine

mf

f

D.C. al Fine

Romanian Song

Arr.: E. Weinzierl / E. Waechter

Moderato

Pretty Minka

Russian Song
Arr.: E. Weinzierl / E. Waechter

Adagio

Mary and Martha

African-American Spiritual
Arr.: E. Weinzierl / E. Waechter

Andante

Sy. 2925

Sleigh Ride
from KV 605

Wolfgang Amadeus Mozart (1756–1791)
Arr.: E. Weinzierl / E. Waechter

Moderato

Chichico

Brazilian Song
Arr.: E. Weinzierl / E. Waechter

Practice tempo: Allegro moderato
Performance tempo: Allegro

Percussive Tones (beat boxing)

Allegro
Op. 149, No. 13

Anton Diabelli (1781–1858)
Arr.: E. Weinzierl / E. Waechter

Practice tempo: Moderato
Performance tempo: Allegro

* Use the rests to slide to the other thumb key: Start with the double thumb key (DTK), change to the single thumb key (STK) in measure eight, and switch back to the double thumb key in measure sixteen.

Allegro

Practice tempo: Moderato
Performance tempo: Allegro

Johann Baptist Vanhal (1739–1831)
Arr.: E. Weinzierl / E. Waechter

Standin' in the Need of Prayer

African-American Spiritual
Arr.: E. Weinzierl / E. Waechter

Andantino
from Op. 211

Cornelius Gurlitt (1820–1901)
Arr.: E. Weinzierl / E. Waechter

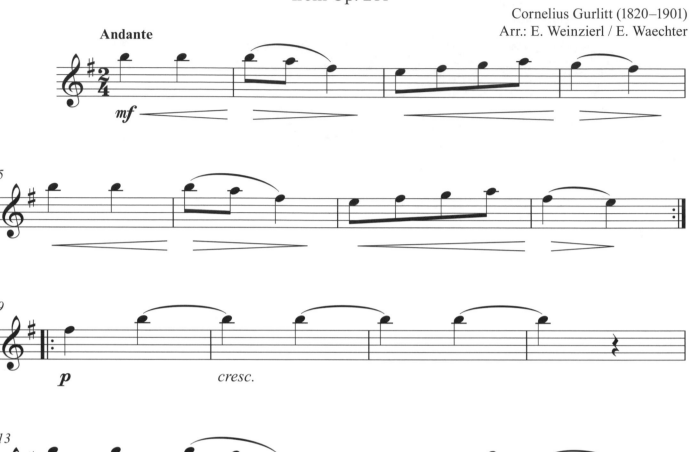

Let's Play Flute! Method Book 1, Chapter 10   Sy. 2925   © 2015 by G. Ricordi & Co., Berlin

French Dance
(Branle)

Nicolas Chédeville (1705–1782)
Arr.: E. Weinzierl / E. Waechter

Let's Play Flute! Method Book 1, Chapter 11   Sy. 2925   © 2015 by G. Ricordi & Co., Berlin

London's Burning
Canon

English Song
(Allegedly written after the Great Fire of London in 1666)
Arr.: E. Weinzierl / E. Waechter

Sur le pont d'Avignon

French Song
Arr.: E. Weinzierl / E. Waechter

14

"From the New World"
from the second movement of Symphony No. 9 in E minor, Op. 95

Antonín Dvořák (1841–1904)
Arr.: E. Weinzierl / E. Waechter

The Wild Horseman
from *Album for the Young,* Op. 68

Practice tempo: Largo
Performance tempo: Adagio

Robert Schumann (1810–1856)
Arr.: E. Weinzierl / E. Waechter

Standin' in the Need of Prayer

African-American Spiritual
Arr.: E. Weinzierl / E. Waechter

Andantino
from Op. 211

Cornelius Gurlitt (1820–1901)
Arr.: E. Weinzierl / E. Waechter

Let's Play Flute! Method Book 1, Chapter 10

French Dance
(Branle)

Nicolas Chédeville (1705–1782)
Arr.: E. Weinzierl / E. Waechter

Let's Play Flute! Method Book 1, Chapter 11   Sy. 2925

London's Burning
Canon

English Song
(Allegedly written after the Great Fire of London in 1666)
Arr.: E. Weinzierl / E. Waechter

Sur le pont d'Avignon

French Song
Arr.: E. Weinzierl / E. Waechter

"From the New World"
from the second movement of Symphony No. 9 in E minor, Op. 95

Antonín Dvořák (1841–1904)
Arr.: E. Weinzierl / E. Waechter

The Wild Horseman

from *Album for the Young,* Op. 68

Robert Schumann (1810–1856)
Arr.: E. Weinzierl / E. Waechter

Practice tempo: Largo
Performance tempo: Adagio

Sy. 2925